Teaching With Newbery Books

by Christine Boardman Moen

SCHOLASTIC
PROFESSIONAL BOOKS

New York • Toronto • London • Auckland • Sydney

Copyright ©1994 by Christine Boardman Moen
Cover and interior design by Vincent Ceci
ISBN 0-590-49415-3
Printed in USA

12 11 10 9 8 7 6 5 4 3

DEDICATION

This book is lovingly dedicated
to my husband Tom, with whom I take
turns leading and following.

ACKNOWLEDGEMENTS

I thank the following people who helped in ways both big and small: Rochelle Murray and her staff at the Davenport Public Library, Tami Chumbley, Children's Services Manager of the Bettendorf Public Library, the wonderful reference librarians and staff members of the Bettendorf Public Library, Greg Bouljon of Bettendorf Middle School, Louise Jesson of Pleasant View Elementary School, and Dr. Harvey A. Daniels, Professor of Education at National-Louis University in Evanston, Illinois.

CONTENTS

INTRODUCTION

*T*eaching with Newbery Books combines compelling literature with interesting instructional approaches to help you and your students join forces to create a literate community in love with reading!

In the chapters that follow, you'll learn how you can select and use nearly 100 Newbery titles (representing almost one-third of the entire Newbery collection) in your classroom to meet curricular needs and to spark student interest and enthusiasm for reading. Instructional approaches include literature circles, genre studies, and author studies as well as whole-group instruction and independent reading programs.

Each discussion presents strategies for using this diverse collection of award-winning children's literature and background information on several titles you might like to use. Extension activities to take students' reading further and suggestions for your own professional reading are sprinkled throughout. Finally, to facilitate your efforts to integrate Newbery books into your classroom, you'll find a complete list (by author) of titles mentioned in this book.

CHAPTER ONE

11

Choosing Newbery Books for Your Classroom

More than 300 books have received the Newbery Medal or Honor since the award was first presented in 1922. Consequently, within the Newbery collection you will find books to match almost every student's literary taste and reading ability. Student readers can enjoy the simplicity of Hugh Lofting's *The Voyages of Dr. Dolittle*, the sophistication of Bruce Brooks' *The Moves Make the Man*, and the gentle humor of Beverly Cleary's *Ramona Quimby, Age 8*. There are picture books such as William Steig's *Doctor De Soto* and Mavis Jukes' *Like Jake and Me* in the collection as well. At the same time, student readers can solve a mystery in *The Westing Game*, experience other worlds in *The Dark is Rising*, and win a prestigious horse race in *King of the Wind*!

The collection also contains a variety of genres that can be used in cross-curricular ways. For example, you might use the non-fiction book *Sugaring Time* in a science unit, *Commodore Perry in the Land of the Shogun* in a social studies unit, and Johanna Reiss' autobiographies *The Upstairs Room* and *The Journey Back* in a history unit. The Newbery collection also includes science fiction books such as *A Wrinkle in Time*, historical fiction such as *Number the Stars*, and biographies such as *The Wright Brothers: How They Invented the Airplane*.

Finally, one of the most appealing aspects of using Newbery books in the classroom is that the collection is ethnically and culturally rich. For example, readers learn about Native American culture and legends in *Anpao: An American Indian Odyssey*, meet the proud African-American Logan family in *Roll of Thunder, Hear My Cry*, and come face-to-face with duty and personal honor in a Spanish bullfight in *Shadow of a Bull*. Students can spend time in Shora, Holland, in *The Wheel on the School*, the Cholistan Desert of Pakistan in *Shabanu: Daughter of the Wind* and explore a Polynesian island in *Call It Courage*.

CONSIDERATIONS WHEN CHOOSING NEWBERY BOOKS

The first person you may want to consider when selecting books for your classroom is yourself. Your own enthusiasm for titles you select can inspire the same in your students. Are you fond of historical fiction? Then you won't want to miss *The Sign of the Beaver*, *Johnny Tremain* or the biographical fiction, *Carry on, Mr. Bowditch*. Are you an adventure enthusiast? If so, you might want to read *Hatchet* or *The True Confession of Charlotte Doyle*. Is having an interesting main character important to you as a reader? If so, you'll enjoy *The Great Gilly Hopkins*, *Maniac Magee*, *Sarah, Plain and Tall* and *M.C. Higgins, the Great*. Finally, if the Civil War intrigues you, you'll be interested in *Rifles for Watie*, *Across Five Aprils*, and *To Be a Slave*.

After reflecting on the types of books that appeal to you, you'll want to learn more about the types of books that appeal to your students. If you have an independent reading program in place in your classroom, you can check students' reading logs to see what types of books appear most frequently on their lists. (Suggestions for including Newbery books in your independent reading program appear in Chapter 5.) You might also check with your librarian or media specialist as well as other teachers for other types of books that appeal to students of the age group of your class. Finally, you can invite students to list types of books and authors they read most fequently or the types of books and names of authors other students recommend to them most often.

CONNECTIONS TO CURRICULUM AREAS

Now that you have a better idea of your own interests and your students' interests, you can take a look at your curriculum to plan connections. Following are a few examples of the different ways you might connect Newbery books to your curriculum.

(For more information on developing themes and setting up literature circles and author studies see Chapters 2 and 3.)

Curriculum Area: Language Arts/First-Person Narrative

Newbery Book: *Philip Hall Likes Me. I Reckon Maybe*

This story is told in the first person, and that person happens to be Elizabeth Lorraine Lambert, otherwise known as Beth, a spirited eleven-year old growing up in rural Arkansas. She is the smartest girl in class and has a crush on the smartest boy in class, Philip Hall. Beth opens a vegetable stand, leads a crusade for the Pretty Pennies, and rescues Philip Hall during the church picnic.

Curriculum Area: Language Arts/Poetry

Newbery Book: *Joyful Noise: Poems for Two Voices*

This sensational volume of poetry recreates the "joyful noise" of insects. Written to be read aloud by two readers at once, you and your students will delight in such poems as "Honeybees," a poem about the very different lives of two honeybees, one a worker and the other a queen. Or you might wish to experience life as a book dweller in "Book Lice" or experience the energetic, acquatic life in "Water Boatmen."

Curriculum Area: Language Arts/Biography

Newbery Book: *Lincoln: A Photobiography*

Using photographs and illustrations, including those of documents and artifacts, Russell Freedman introduces students to the 16th president of the United States. While exploring Lincoln's life and career, Freedman also provides an effective, readable description of the issues surrounding Lincoln and a country divided by civil war.

Curriculum Area: Science

Newbery Book: *Volcano: The Eruption and Healing*

of Mount St. Helens

This outstanding photo essay about the 1980 eruption of Mount St. Helens is simply written and easy to understand. The color photographs help illustrate nature's unique ability to restore and heal itself after monumental natural disasters.

Curriculum Area: Geography/Social Studies

Newbery Book: *Commodore Perry in the Land of the Shogun*

In 1853 Commodore Matthew Perry led an American expedition to Japan, the land of the Shogun. This very readable book describes how Americans and Japanese accommodated each other's cultures and finally signed the Treaty of Kanagawa. The book also contains the text of the treaty, a photograph of Commodore Perry, reproductions of Japanese illustrations of the period, and even lists of the gifts the Americans and Japanese exchanged.

Curriculum Area: Art

Newbery Book: *I, Juan De Pareja*

This challenging book, written as an autobiography, is actually a historical novel describing the life of Juan de Pareja. Born a slave in 17th century Spain, Juan de Pareja became the servant of Spanish artist Diego Velazquez, who was court painter for King Philip IV. Although Spanish law forbid slaves such as Juan to learn how to paint, Juan secretly studied and eventually not only became a free man but also a good friend of his former master, Velazquez. Velazquez's portrait of Juan de Pareja hangs in The Metropolitan Museum of Art.

Two of Velazquez's most notable works include "Las Meninas" (in which he includes a self-portrait) and "The Weavers." Juan de Paraja's most notable painting is "The Calling of Saint Matthew" in which he, too, includes a self-portrait. All three portraits and many more of Velazquez's works can be seen in The Metropolitan Museum of Art's 1989 edition of "Velazquez" by Antonio Dominguez Ortiz, Alfonso E. Perez

Sanchez, and Julian Gallego (Abrams, 1989). In addition, Chertok, Hirshfeld, and Rosh's book Meet the Masterpieces *(Scholastic Professional Books, 1992) includes a color poster of "Las Meninas" as well as student activities.*

READING NEWBERY BOOKS ALOUD

When choosing Newbery books to use in your classroom, you might want to select titles that make good read-alouds.

The importance of reading aloud to all students, even students in the upper grades, is supported by Charolotte S. Huck in *Talking About Books*. Huck states: "Reading aloud is important at all levels of education, for it helps provide the motivation for learning to read and reading." Huck also explains that "reading aloud to children develops their vocabulary" and urges teachers "to continue reading aloud to older children in order to motivate them to read or to share a book or poem that they might otherwise miss."

Some ways you can use Newbery books during read-aloud time follow.

To Expand an Author Study

If you are doing an author study and students are reading either the same book or different books by the same author, you may want to read aloud a book by the author that either represents a very different style or contains a new main character. For example, if students are reading the Ramona books by Beverly Cleary, you may want to read *Dear Mr. Henshaw* as it not only has a different main character but also represents a different type of Beverly Cleary book.

As a Way to Explore Themes

Often the same Newbery book can be used to support a variety of themes. For example, you might read aloud *Annie and the Old One* as part of a unit about Native Americans. You can use the same book for a discussion on how people react to death.

You can also select read-alouds that enhance a theme students are exploring in other books they are reading. For instance, if your theme is friendship and your literature circle groups are reading *The Sign of the Beaver*, *Bridge to Terabithia*, and *Philip Hall Likes Me. I Reckon Maybe*, then you might want to read aloud *The Whipping Boy*, which is a humorous look at a friendship that grows out of a unique situation.

As a Way to Pique Interest

Sometimes just reading aloud the first few pages or an especially entertaining episode from a book will get students interested in reading that particular book or perhaps a book by the same author. For example, if you have some sophisticated science fantasy fans in your classroom, you may want to read part of Susan Cooper's *The Dark is Rising*. If you have adventure fans, you may want to read the description in *Call It Courage* of Mafatu's escape from his island with six war canoes full of angry natives in hot pursuit.

Another way to pique interest is to share a recorded adaptation of a particular Newbery book. (An available source of recorded adaptations is listed in this chapter under "Resources to Help You Choose Your Newbery Books.") Many adaptations are enhanced with music and are award-winning recordings. (Don't worry that students might not want to read the books after listening to recorded adaptations. The background knowledge and familiarity the recordings provide can inspire children to pick up books they might not otherwise select.)

As Models of Literary Devices

Because Newbery books represent outstanding writing, it's not difficult to find excellent examples of literary devices to share with students who can then weave the same devices into their own writing. For example, note the use of personification in Cynthia Rylant's *Missing May*: "The capitol building sprawled gray concrete like a regal queen spreading out her petticoats, and its giant dome glittered pure gold in the morning sun. I felt in me an embarrassing sense of pride that she was ours."

AS CROSS-CURRICULAR ENHANCEMENT

In "The Effects of Teaching Reading with Historical Fiction on Elementary Students' Learning of Historical Concepts: A Pilot Study" (*Contemporary Issues in Reading*, Vol. 6, 1990; pages 13-17), John A. Smith, a professor at Utah State University, reports that when students read the Newbery book *Johnny Tremain* while also reading about the Revolutionary War in their social studies text, they were able to recall information about the American Revolution better and read their social studies textbooks with more understanding.

With this reseach in mind, below are just a few of the cross-curricular areas in which you can use Newbery books to enhance your social studies and/or history curricula during read-aloud time:

Curriculum Area: New England in the 1830's

Newbery Book: *A Gathering of Days: A New England Girl's Journal, 1830-32*

Students might hesitate to choose to read this book because of its diary format and its literary style, which is faithful to the 1830's. Read aloud, however, the story of thirteen-year-old Catherine and her encounter with a runaway slave, her adjustment to her stepmother, and the death of her best friend make her life on her New Hampshire farm come alive as if she were the voice of a relative, long since dead but speaking to us today.

Curriculum Area: Slave Trade in America during 1840's

Newbery Book: *The Slave Dancer*

Incredibly powerful, The Slave Dancer *is the story of Jessie Bollier, a thirteen-year-old who is kidnapped from the docks of New Orleans and pressed into service on the illegal slave ship,* The Moonlight. *Jessie witnesses the violent and inhuman conditions of slavery as he is forced to play the fife while the slaves exercise on deck.* Booklist *is accurate in its description of* The Slave Dancer *as being written in "graphic, documentary prose."*

Curriculum Area: Boston in early 1770's prior to Revolutionary War

Newbery Book: *Johnny Tremain*

This popular historical fiction novel tells how Johnny Tremain, after an accident in a silversmith's shop cripples his right hand, becomes involved with Sam Adams, Paul Revere, and John Hancock as he delivers "The Boston Observer" *in pre-American Revolutionary Boston.*

READING ALOUD PREQUELS, SEQUELS, OR SERIES

If students like particular authors or become especially interested in particular characters, they often want to read more books by the same authors or read more books about the same characters. To encourage this continued or "independent" reading habit, you may want to read aloud some of the prequels, sequels, or books in a series related to the books in the Newbery collection.

For a list of suggested titles, see Chapter 5.

OTHER RECOMMENDED BOOKS FOR READING ALOUD

The fourteen books described below are not the only Newbery books that are appropriate for reading aloud. Others you're probably familiar with include *Charlotte's Web, Caddie Woodlawn, Sarah, Plain and Tall, Dear Mr. Henshaw* and *From the Mixed-Up Files of Mrs. Basil E. Frankwiler.* What follows is a good mixture of old and new titles. More importantly, the books described below "talk to" students the way only very good books can by using the language, rhythm, and images that hold students' interest and attention.

GRADES 4, 5, 6

Number the Stars

Ten-year-old Annemarie Johansen lives in Copenhagen, Denmark, in 1943, and the Nazis have begun "relocating" Danish Jews. Annemarie and her family fear for their friends, the Rosens, and decide to risk their own lives to help them escape by smuggling them across the sea to Sweden. This is an incredible story of courage and friendship.

Sounder

A poor black family sharecropping in the rural South is torn apart when the father is arrested for stealing a ham in order to feed his starving family. During the arrest, Sounder, the family's coon dog, is shot and crawls off. In the remainder of the story, the boy (all characters remain nameless except for Sounder) searches for his father, his dog, and a way to educate himself. *Sounder* is an eloquent, emotional book.

The Great Gilly Hopkins

Gilly Hopkins is a character students will long remember. Angry and defiant, Gilly is determined to get the upper hand at her new foster home, the third she's been in in less than three years. However, sarcasm and suspicion turn to love as Trotter, William Ernest, and blind, old Mr. Randolph become Gilly's family—until Gilly's grandmother shows up.

The Hundred Dresses

This simple, yet powerful book is one of the best read-aloud books ever written. Students learn lessons of tolerance and human kindness from Wanda Petronski, a little Polish girl who is tormented by her classmates when she says she has a hundred dresses lined up in her closet.

Thimble Summer

Every child should have a "thimble summer" where dreams come true and everything turns out wonderfully. In this happy book, nine-year-old Garnet Linden has a golden summer on her Midwestern farm.

Blue Willow

For Janey, who is an only child and the daughter of migrant workers, the only constant, unchangeable thing in her life is her cherished blue-willow plate which had belonged to her mother. Despite Bounce Reyburn's thievery and her stepmother's illness, Janey finds a permanent home where her family can stay "as long as we want to."

Incident at Hawk's Hill

Based on a true incident that occurred in June 1870 on the Manitoba prairie lands of Canada, *Incident at Hawk's Hill* is the story of six-year-old Ben MacDonald who wanders off and is "adopted" by a female badger whose own litter has starved to death. Ben is found after two months, and the once uncomfortable relationship with his father comes to full understanding after a tragedy brings them closer together.

GRADES 6,7,8

Roll of Thunder, Hear My Cry

The Logans, a black family living in Mississippi, own their own land—something that was very rare during the Depression of the 1930's and something that gives the Logans dignity while causing jealousy and hatred in others. It is the jealousy and hatred that the Logans, and especially eleven-year-old Cassie, must endure in order to maintain their independence and humanity.

Maniac Magee

Maniac Magee—alias Jeffrey Lionel Magee—becomes a legend in Two Mills, as he teaches the white kids from the East End and the black kids from the West End to get along. The pace of the story is as fast as Maniac's running, and the dialogue and characterizations are brutally realistic. At the same time, the story retains some of the qualities of old-fashioned tall tales.

The True Confession of Charlotte Doyle

This wonderful adventure story is told in the first person as thirteen-year-old Charlotte Doyle tells of her Atlantic Ocean crossing aboard the ship *Seahawk* in the summer of 1832. Although Charlotte's boarding school training does not prepare her for the rigors of sea life, she nevertheless stands up to a ruthless captain, wins the loyalty of a mutinous crew, and clears herself of a murder charge.

M.C. Higgins, the Great

This powerful novel introduces students to thirteen-year-old Mayo Cornelius Higgins whose family has lived on Sarah's Mountain in the Appalachians since his great-grandmother Sarah, a former slave, settled there. Strip mining has come to Sarah's Mountain, and M.C. fears the heap of debris poised dangerously above his home. M.C. longs to leave the mountain, but he knows Jones, his father, is tied to the mountain because of the past. In the end it is those ties to the past that give M.C. hope for the future.

Banner in the Sky

In the author's notes to *Banner in the Sky*, James Ramsey Ullman states that "there are many ways in which this story resembles the true story of the first climbing of the Matterhorn." He adds that the story in *Banner in the Sky* "branches out on its own trail, to its own mountaintop." What results is an exciting story of sixteen-year-old Rudi Matt of Kurtal whose father died trying to climb the Citadel, the loftiest mountain peak in Switzerland. Rudi does climb the Citadel, however, and demonstrates the courage and kindness of his legendary father.

The Westing Game

Keeping track of all the clues and the cast of characters will be part of the fun of reading this book aloud. Intricate in detail and dripping with clues, your students will have fun with this play-along mystery story. (Note: Make sure you read this yourself before reading aloud so *you* know what's going on!)

Across Five Aprils

This beautifully written story is the saga of the Creighton family as it experiences five Aprils during the Civil War. Young Jethro Creighton is left behind on the family's Illinois farm as the Civil War ravages families, the nation, and its leaders. Especially touching is President Lincoln's letter to young Ceighton regarding the status of deserters.

STUDENT READ ALOUDS: READERS' THEATRE

Students can become a part of the read-aloud experience by participating in readers' theatre. In readers' theatre, students play different parts including that of the narrator. To involve as many students as possible, pair students for each part. Students can then choose to read together or take turns.

Prepare for a readers' theatre experience by reading the book aloud first so everyone is familiar with the story. To help students anticipate their lines, indicate parts in pencil by starring, underlining, or flagging with different colored stick-on notes.

Although almost any book lends itself to readers' theatre, the following titles are especially effective:

The Hundred Penny Box

Great-great Aunt Dew has come to live with Michael and his family. Michael loves Aunt Dew's singing and especially loves the stories that she tells while going through the sack of pennies in her hundred penny box. Michael's practical mother wants to get rid of Aunt Dew's hundred penny box, but Michael protests. He's heard Aunt Dew say, "I got to keep looking at my box and when I don't see my box I won't see me neither."

Nothing But the Truth

Described as a "documentary novel" and written in play format, *Nothing But the Truth* will have students debating respect, freedom, and patriotism while discussing point of view and characterization. As the book's introduction states, your

students will have the facts but "the truth—and nothing but the truth—can be discovered by only one person: the reader."

RESOURCES TO HELP YOU SELECT BOOKS

You might find the following resources helpful as you incorporate Newbery books in your classroom:

The New York Times' Parent's Guide to the Best Books for Children (revised and updated) by Eden Ross Lipson (Random House, 1991)

Lipson gives short, helpful synopses of hundreds of different books, including more than 75 Newbery Award and Honor books.

American Library Association Best of the Best for Children by Denise Perry Donavin (Random House, 1992)

Donavin, too, gives short, helpful synopses of hundreds of books, including descriptions of many Newbery Award and Honor books.

Handbook for the Newbery Medal and Honor Books, 1980-1989 by Bette D. Ammon and Gale W. Sherman (Freline, 1991)

Ammon and Sherman provide plot summaries, read-aloud tips, cross-curricular ideas, and recommended reading lists for all 36 Newbery Medal and Honor Books from 1980 to 1989.

Newbery Medal Books, 1922-1955 edited by Bertha Mahony Miller and Elinor Whitney Field

Newbery and Caldecott Medal Books, 1966-1975 edited by Bertha Mahony Miller and Elinor Whitney Field

Newbery and Caldecott Medal Books, 1976-1985 edited by Lee Kingman

These books contain descriptions and excerpts of Newbery Medal books and biographies of the authors and their winning speeches. For more information contact: The Horn Book, Inc., 14 Beacon Street HB, Boston, MA 02108 (1-800-325-1170).

RECORDED ADAPTATIONS

Adaptations of many Newbery books are available on tape from SRA, a division of Macmillan/McGraw-Hill. To request a media catalog call 1-800-843-8855 or write P.O. Box 544, Blacklick, Ohio 43004-0544.

CHAPTER TWO

Literature
Circles

WHAT IS A LITERATURE CIRCLE?

A literature circle is a group of 3-5 students gathered together to discuss the book they are reading or have just finished reading. Most often, all the students in the same group have read or are reading the same book, although there are times when students who have read different books that have similar characteristics may wish to form literature circles. (Also called author studies and genre studies, these kinds of groups are discussed in chapter 3.)

WHY USE LITERATURE CIRCLES?

Dorothy J. Watson writes: In "Show Me: Whole Language Evaluation of Literature Groups" (*Talking About Books*), "One of the goals of literature study is to provide a setting in which students and teachers are secure and comfortable in sharing their intellectual and emotional connections with literature. Students' personal meanings that are created while reading alone are deepened through the social transaction within a group of learners."

An extension of Watson's statement is that the overall purpose of literature circles is to promote reading by creating literate communities within the classroom. Thus, students who form these mini-literate communities or literature circles respond personally to literature as they construct meaning from text.

Do literature circles promote reading? Fifth grade teacher Marianne Flanagan describes her experiences with literature circles in "Starting Literature Circles in Fifth Grade": "The power of the literature groups has instilled in the students an incredible thirst for reading." (Best Practice 2, Chicago Project on Learning and Teaching; National University Press, 1991)

Classrooms often have 3 to 5 different literature circles going at the same time. Each circle reads a different book from a text set (a group of different books related to a theme.) For example, with a text set based on a theme such as "Animals as Friends," the literature circles might look like this:

Group A *Rascal*
Group B *Old Yeller*
Group C *Shiloh*
Group D *King of the Wind*

Each Group A member receives a copy of Rascal, *each Group B member reads* Old Yeller, *and so on. Other characteristics of literature circles include the following:*

1. Discussion groups are temporary and are formed based upon book choice.

2. Students select the book they wish to read. When creating text sets, try to represent both students' interests and reading abilities. For example, using the text set "Animals as Friends," *Rascal*, the story of a young boy and his pet raccoon, is longer and more challenging than *Shiloh*, a story about a boy and a dog he rescues from abuse. However, although *Shiloh* is a shorter, less difficult book to read, it's immensely satisfying. Students who love books about horses might want to read *King of the Wind* while the heart-warming *Old Yeller* may appeal to students who are interested in a story about a family's love for a special dog.

3. Groups schedule discussion time and meet regularly—(Aim for 30 minutes, three times a week.)

4. New groups form when new book choices are made within an established text set and/or when a new text set is introduced to explore a new theme.

5. The teacher models different literature circle roles (see pages 31-33) when the groups first begin meeting. Once students become familiar with the different roles, the teacher becomes observer-evaluator and problem-solver facilitator.

6. Although literary analysis is a significant focus of literature circle discussions, each student's personal response to the literature is the point at which discussion begins.

MANAGING LITERATURE CIRCLES

As with other literature-based and whole language strategies, there is not one definitive way to manage and conduct literature circles in your classroom.

As you experiment and adapt the circles to suit your particular classroom and environment, you might find the following guidelines helpful:

• Pique your students' interest in each of the books in the text set by giving a book talk. Read aloud a portion of the book, act out a scene from the book, compare and contrast the book with others students have read, show art work, describe the mood.

• Create a lottery system whereby students take turns choosing the books they wish to read when you introduce the text set. Remember that in order to accommodate students' choices, you'll want to be sure to have 5 or 6 copies of each book in your text set. Still, students may not get their first book choices. You might keep a list and allow those students to get first choice from the same text set when the literature circles re-form.

•Let the type of discussion you want determine the size of literature circles. Keep in mind that the size of the groups will affect conversational dynamics. Large groups tend to discuss more topics and to provide a larger number of different perspectives. Discussion is often fast paced. Smaller groups typically discuss fewer topics and provide fewer perspectives, but individual group members have the opportunity to develop their individual perspectives more fully.

•Plan for group closure. As a class management aid, you might plan for each group to finish reading the books on a common date. Thus, at each group's first meeting, members can "chunk out" their book and decide how much they'll read each day in order to meet the target date. As the group progresses through the book, members can decide if at some point they would like to read with a partner.

•Plan appropriate reading and writing mini-lessons.

Encourage students to discuss the literary devices and practice using them in their own writing by introducing and showing examples of literary elements from their books. (When you find examples of literary devices or passages that demonstrate outstanding dialogue or description, you might attach a "stick-on" note on the page and label. Encourage students to do the same.)

LITERATURE CIRCLE ROLES

In his book *Collaborative Reading: Literature Circles and Text Sets in the Classroom* (in press), Harvey Daniels creates a number of role sheets that students can use when preparing for and participating in literature circles.

Daniels states: "These roles not only provide structure when the group meets, they also affect kids' reading processes because each role sets a very definite purpose for reading. Further, when kids have worked through a couple of cycles, playing each different role a few times, they internalize the habits each role promotes—they virtually cannot stop themselves from looking at texts in the four or five ways they have learned."

Following are names and descriptions of some of these literature circle roles:

Discussion Director

The discussion director develops a list of questions the group might want to discuss, focusing on main ideas from the reading, how the book relates to the major concepts of the theme, and students' reactions to the book. (You might model how to ask open-ended questions as opposed to single-response questions and invite students to give examples of each.)
(Note: Theme concepts are discussed later in this chapter.)

Vocabulary Enricher

The vocabulary enricher helps bring the group's attention to unfamiliar words or important words in the text that may be

repeated a lot, used in unusual ways, or are key to the meaning of the day's reading. The vocabulary enricher points these words out in the book during the discussion and shares their definitions.

Literary Luminary (Passage Master)

The literary luminary selects special passages or sections of the text to read aloud or read again silently when the group meets. These passages are memorable or significant in some way (for example, sad, funny, or dramatic). The literary luminary may decide to read the passages aloud or have someone else read the passages aloud before the group discusses each passage.

Process Checker

The process checker keeps track of each member's participation and during the last few minutes of the group's discussion, reviews the group's meeting and writes comments about each member's contribution. The process checker also records any group highlights or problems that occurred during the day's meeting.

Connector

The connector points out to the group any connections the day's reading has with other material the class has read, school or community events, or to life and the world in general. In other words, the connector points out the connections between the literature and the students in the group.

Although Dr. Daniels suggests a number of other roles for literature circles, the above represent some of the basic roles you may find useful in your own classroom. Ready-to-Use Role Sheets are available in Dr. Daniels' book, but you can also create your own role sheets.

When creating your own role sheets, keep in mind the uniqueness of the literature your students are reading. For example, if your groups are reading Russell Freedman's *Lincoln: A Photobiography*, you may want a student to serve as Time Liner. This student would be responsible for creating a time line of Lincoln's life that also includes the historical events that took place during his life. Groups can display their time lines on the classroom wall when the literature circles finish. (Note: *Timeliner* software by Tom Snyder Productions is easy to use and prints banner-size time lines.)

Another role that students might play when appropriate is Map Maker. For example, if students are reading Rhoda Blumberg's *Commodore Perry in the Land of the Shogun,* the map maker would be responsible for creating maps or adding to the group's map to accompany the day's discussion.

TEXT SETS AND ACCOMPANYING THEMES

Theme units are based on major concepts that become mental templates or frameworks that can shape and hold literature circle discussions. In *Invitations: Changing as Teachers and Learners K-12* (Heinemenn, 1991), Regie Routman differentiates between themes and what she calls "correlations"—activities related to topics such as bears, insects, or careers.

As the following example shows, Newbery books can help you weave correlations and thematic concepts together using a literature circle approach.

THEME 1-ANIMALS AS FRIENDS

Correlation: Main characters and their pet animals

Major Concept: In many ways, animals fulfill the qualities of friendship the same way humans do. Subpoints:

Animal friends can take on human qualities.

Human friends have special responsibilities towards their animal friends.

TEXT SET:

Rascal by Sterling North

In the first sentence of his book, Sterling North describes his pet raccoon Rascal as "a character, a personality, and a ring-tailed wonder." *Rascal* is based on North's childhood and describes how Rascal became a part of his life for one memorable year in 1918.

Old Yeller by Fred Gipson

Fourteen-year-old Travis wants nothing to do with the big, dingy yellow stray dog that steals meat one night from the family. Travis has enough to do working the farm in the Texas hill country while his father is off driving their cattle to Kansas. But Old Yeller does become a part of the family—even after his death.

Shiloh by Phyllis Reynolds Naylor

Eleven-year-old Marty Preston knows that where he comes from, people mind their own business. But when Marty learns that Judd Travers is abusing his dog Shiloh, he decides "there's got to be times that what one person does is everybody's business." And so Marty sets out to make Shiloh his own.

King of the Wind by Marguerite Henry

Agba, the mute Moroccan stableboy, promises Sham, the newborn foal, that he will never abandon him. Thus Agba and Sham are destined to live through hardships as well as glory as they travel from Morocco to France and finally to England where Sham is crowned King of the Wind. (The story is based on the legend of the thoroughbred sire, Godolphin Arabian.)

◆◆◆◆◆◆◆◆◆◆◆◆◆◆◆◆◆◆◆◆◆◆

By extending the "correlation" and theme of Animals as Friends to include the major concept of how animals fulfill the qualities of friendship the same way humans do, students extend the story in the text and connect it to the much larger concept of the qualities of friendship.

Major concepts and subpoints can be introduced to students before literature circles begin. Discussion Directors and Connectors can remind students of the major concept and subpoints and help focus the group's attention on them.

FINAL LITERATURE CIRCLE DISCUSSION/ACTIVITY

When your class is finished with the text set, a final activity is to re-form literature circles with at least one student who has read *Rascal*, another student who has read *Shiloh*, and so on. In their new groups, encourage students to make connections between all four books and explain how each relates to the major concept and the subpoints. Invite each group to share a summary of its discussion with the class.

ADDITIONAL THEMES, CONCEPTS, AND TEXT SETS

The remainder of this chapter presents three additional themes. Keep in mind that the Newbery collection of books is quite large and versatile. The same books can support a variety of themes and concepts and can be used in a number of different text sets. Thus the suggestions that follow simply represent a place for you to start.

THEME 2 - SURVIVAL

Correlation: Main characters that demonstrate courage and survival skills

Major Concept: People have an instinct to survive.

Subpoints: Surviving in nature requires people to understand nature.
                        Surviving in nature requires people to understand their own strengths and weaknesses.

TEXT SET:

Julie of the Wolves by Jean Craghead George
Thirteen-year-old Julie, an Eskimo girl also known as Miyax, survives on the tundra when she is protected and cared for by Amaroq, a fearless wolf. This is also a story about the Eskimo culture and Julie's struggle for self-identify.

Hatchet by Gary Paulsen
Thirteen-year-old Brian Robeson is heading for the oil fields of Canada to spend the summer with his father when the pilot of his small Cessna 406 has a heart attack and dies seven thousand feet in the air. The hatchet Brian's mother gave him as a going-away gift and his courage help Brian survive for nearly two months in the wilderness.

Call It Courage by Armstrong Sperry
Twelve-year-old Mafatu's name means "Stout Heart," but the other people on his Polynesian island call him a coward because he fears the sea after witnessing his mother being swept away during a hurricane. Alone with his dog Uri, Mafatu sets out to find his courage as he survives a storm at sea and life on a strange island.

My Side of the Mountain by Jean Craighead George
Sam Girbly left New York City with a penknife, a ball of cord, an ax, some flint and steel, and forty dollars. He was determined to live in a tree house in the Catskill Mountains. His experiences with nature and his ability to survive make this a wonderful story.

FINAL LITERATURE CIRCLE DISCUSSION/ACTIVITY

When students finish with the text set, re-form literature circles so that each circle has students who have read at least one of the different books in the text set. Focus discussion on how all four books relate to the major concept: people have instincts to survive and that in order to survive, people need to understand nature and themselves.

Share newspaper and news magazine articles describing real-life instances where people have survived in the wilderness or at sea.

As a final writing activity, invite students to write newspaper accounts of survival stories they read about in their books, for example for *Julie of the Wolves*: ESKIMO GIRL SURVIVES TUNDRA Wolf Pack Saves Her Life and *Hatchet*: BOY SURVIVES PLANE CRASH Spends Two Months Alone in Wilderness.

THEME 3 - FAMILY

Correlation: The influence of family on main characters

Major Concept: Each of us accepts and rejects our family's influence as we grow in self-understanding.

Subpoints: Fathers influence us even when they are absent.
As members of a family, we have responsibilities to our families but also responsibilities to ourselves.

TEXT SET:

Shadow of a Bull by Maia Wojciechowska

Eleven-year-old Manolo Olivar is terrified to follow in the footsteps of his famous bullfighting father, who was killed in the arena. Although pressured by others to be just like his father because "the art of bullfighting is dying and we need someone to bring it back to life," Manola learns he really does have a choice about his life.

My Brother Sam is Dead by James Lincoln Collier and Christopher Collier

Tim Meeker is torn between his Tory father and his brother Sam, who is fighting with the American Revolutionary Army. This is a powerful story about family loyalty.

The Summer of the Swans by Betsy Byars

Just the day before, fourteen-year-old Sara Godfrey had been confused about herself, annoyed by her brain-damaged brother and her Aunt Willie, angry at her father, and even angrier at Joe Melby. All that changes on one summer's day.

Onion John by Joseph Krumgold

Andy Rusch wants to spend the summer working along side his father in their hardware store and spending time with his friend, Onion John, a superstitious immigrant handyman who lives in a tumble-down house with four bathtubs in his living room. Andy's father, however, has different plans not only for Andy's future but for Onion John's as well.

FINAL LITERATURE CIRCLE DISCUSSION/ACTIVITY

When students finish with the text set, re-form literature circles so that each circle has students who have read at least one of the different books in the text set. Ask each new group to discuss the major concept: the main characters in the stories accepted and rejected the influence of their families as they grew up and learned about themselves.

As a final writing activity, students can identify some of the influences their own families have on them. They can explain how they accept or reject these influences.

THEME 4 - FRIENDSHIPS

Correlation: Friendships of Main Characters

Major Concept:	Friendships change as the people within the friendships change and grow up.
Subpoints:	Trust and loyalty are important in friendships. Friends have a variety of ways of showing their friendship.

TEXT SET:

Dear Mr. Henshaw by Beverly Cleary

Leigh Botts is a sixth grader who has moved to a new town and is attending a new school. He writes letters to his favorite author, Mr. Henshaw, and describes the longing he has for his absent father. As Leigh grows, the letters become diary entries.

The Whipping Boy by Sid Fleischman

When Prince Brat refuses to learn his lessons or plays pranks, Jemmy, the whipping boy, is punished. When Prince Brat runs away and takes Jemmy with him, the roles are reversed when the ruffian Hold-Your-Nose Billy catches them. In the end, however, friendship prevails, and Jemmy and the Prince face the king together.

The Sign of the Beaver by Elizabeth George Speare

Twelve-year-old Matt is left alone to tend the family's new cabin in the Maine wilderness while his father returns to Massachusetts to fetch the rest of the family. Matt is rescued by an Indian chief and his grandson Attean, who reluctantly agrees to learn English from Matt while he teaches Matt how to survive in the wilderness.

The Egypt Game by Zilpha Keatley Snyder

When April first came to live with her grandmother at the Casa Rosada Apartments, she was determined to be as aloof and sophisticated as her would-be actress mother. But that was before she met Melanie and they started the Egypt Game. This is the story of make-believe fun, friendship, and mystery.

FINAL LITERATURE CIRCLE DISCUSSION/ACTIVITY

Re-form groups so that each circle has students in it who have each read a different book in the text set. Focus the discussion on how all four of the books relate to the major concept: friendships change and grow as the people within the friendships change and grow.

As a final writing activity, students can describe how a friendship of their own has changed for the better or for the worse over a period of time.

CHAPTER THREE

Genre Studies and Author Studies

GENRE STUDIES USING NEWBERY BOOKS

A genre study is exactly that—a study of literature as it relates to a particular genre. In a genre study, students in literature circles read books that can be classified as fantasy, historical fiction, biography, poetry, mystery, and adventure, to name just a few of the many categories.

Books organized by genre share certain characteristics. For example, *Caddie Woodlawn* is a historical fiction novel because it is based on a real person and real events, but the details of the action and conversations are fictitious. On the other hand, *Lincoln: A Photobiography* is considered a biography because it is a factual account of Lincoln's life.

ORGANIZING GENRE STUDIES

Organizing a genre study is similar to organizing a theme study. (For more information on organizing text sets around themes, see Chapter 2.) However, instead of focusing discussion around a major concept, students discuss how the book fits the characteristics of a particular genre (in addition, of course, to discussing the book itself using the literature circle roles).

As a preliminary activity, you might discuss the characteristics of the particular genre and share examples before introducing the text set.

Following are examples of genre studies with text set suggestions. Of course, you'll want to include your favorite Newbery books whenever they fit.

Note: One way to organize a genre study is to have each literature circle study a different genre and then share a final project with the class as a culminating activity. Organizing a genre study this way requires a bit more preparation, but allows for the most reader choice.

Genre: Fantasy and Science Fiction

Fantasy books have talking animals, supernatural beings, and parallel worlds woven together in a time and place where all the story elements seem possible. Science fiction, on the other hand, is fantasy with a scientific twist. Science fiction stories will often manipulate time as fantasy stories do, but science fiction stories are usually based on advanced, unknown technology. (Note: Members of some communitiies object to any mention of fantasy or science fiction. Let your principal or colleagues guide you in deciding whether to tackle this genre.)

Characteristics
- Talking animals, as in *Charlotte's Web*
- Supernatural beings, as in *The Black Cauldron*
- Parallel worlds, as in *A Swiftly Tilting Planet*
- Advanced, unknown technology, as in *A Wrinkle in Time.*
- The impossible becomes possible, as in *The Twenty-One Balloons* and *Mr. Popper's Penguins*
- The manipulation of time, as in *The Dark is Rising*

TEXT SET:

A Wrinkle in Time by Madeleine L'Engle
In this classic story of good and evil, Meg Murry and her brother Charles Wallace travel to Camazotz to rescue their father from IT. Not only do they learn what a tesseract is (a wrinkle in time), they also learn that like and equal are not the same thing. (Note: This is the first book in L'Engle's Time series. Other titles are noted in the final chapter of this book.)

The High King by Lloyd Alexander
This finale to the Chronicles of Prydain is a story about good vs. evil. Drnwyn, the most powerful weapon in the kingdom, is stolen by Arawn, Lord of Annuvin, Land of the Dead. To escape annihilation, Taran, Princess Eilonwy, and their companions must march to Annuvin and fight. (Note: For a less ambitious book in this same series, try *The Black Cauldron*.)

Mrs. Frisby and the Rats of NIMH by Robert C. O'Brien
Twenty educated rats who have escaped from NIMH (National Institute of Mental Health) offer to help Mrs. Frisby. They also share with her their Plan for the future: to be self-sufficient by growing their own crops. (The sequels are *Rasco and the Rats of NIMH* and *R-T, Margaret, and the Rats of NIMH* written by Jane Conly, the author's daughter.)

Note: The above text set is suitable for more mature readers. A suitable fantasy-only text set for younger readers might include *Charlotte's Web*, *Mr. Popper's Penguins*, and *Rabbit Hill*.

Culminating Activities
- Have students create time lines that plot inventions and technological breakthroughs in science and medicine.
- Have students suggest possible technology for the future and describe its advantages and disadvantages.
- Have students write descriptions of fantasy lands or kingdoms and describe the characters (human and/or animal) that populate it.

Genre: Historical Fiction
Historical fiction makes a particular time period and the people and events of that time period come alive by fictionalizing actual historical events that tell the reader the way things might have been. Historical accuracy is important in historical fiction even though the conversations of characters are usually fictitious.

Characteristics
- In some stories, the main character actually lived, as in *Caddie Woodlawn*
- In some stories, the main characters are fictitious but based on people who actually lived, as in *Dragonwings*
- In some stories, the main characters are fictitious but other characters within the story actually lived, as in *Johnny Tremain*
- The stories are based on historical events or incidents, as in *Incident at Hawk's Hill*.
- The historical details may be accurate, as in *My Brother Sam Is Dead*

TEXT SET:

Dragonwings by Laurence Yep
Yep calls *Dragonwings* a historical fantasy based on an actual newspaper account of Fung Joe Guey who flew in the

hills of Oakland, California, for twenty minutes on September 22, 1909. In *Dragonwings*, eight-year-old Moon Shadow travels from China and joins his father Windrider in San Francisco. Moon Shadow helps his father achieve his dream of flight despite racial prejudice, extreme poverty, and the 1906 San Francisco earthquake.

Caddie Woodlawn by Carol Ryrie Brink

Based on the real-life adventures of Caddie Woodlawn who lived near Menomonie, Wisconsin, during the Civil War, Caddie lives the pioneer life and even prevents a confrontation between the settlers and the Chippewa Indian Tribe. She learns that "life is just a lot of everyday adventures." (Note: Caddie Woodlawn was the author's real-life grandmother.)

Carry On, Mr. Bowditch by Jean Lee Latham

Latham calls *Carry On, Mr. Bowditch* a "fictionalized biography." This story is based on the real life of Nathaniel Bowditch who sailed on clipper ships in the late 1700's, discovered a new method of celestial navigation, and wrote *The American Practical Navigator*, which became known as "the sailor's Bible."

CULMINATING ACTIVITIES

- Have students select historical events and read about them. Next, have students write conversations that might have taken place between people involved in the events.
- Invite students to act out scenes from their books.
- Have students write newspaper accounts of events that take place in their books.

Genre: Folktales

Folktales are often humorous and usually contain characters that are one-dimensional. In other words, the characters are often entirely good, bad, lazy, and so on. At the same time, folktales sometimes attempt to explain nature or human beings and the culture in which they live. Folktales sometimes include the supernatural.

Characteristics

- In some folktales, nature is explained as in "The Lessons of Heaven and Earth" from *Anpao.*
- Characters are often one-dimensional, for example the amiable fool in "When Shlemiel Went to Warsaw" from *When Shlemiel Went to Warsaw and Other Stories* or the foolish trickster Anansi in "Anansi's Fishing Expedition" from *The Cow-Tail Switch and Other West African Stories*.
- Tales often reward good and punish evil as in "A Tale of Three Tails" from *Tales from Silver Lands*.
- Tales often comment about human nature as in "The Tale of the Lazy People" from *Tales from Silver Lands.*
- Some tales have wizards and witches as in "A Tale of Three Tails" in *Tales from Silver Lands*. (When magic is added to a folktale, it can then be considered a fairy tale.) Other tales include the supernatural as in "The Woman in the Snow" from *The Dark-Thirty*.
- Some tales explain the origin of things as in "Chop-Sticks" from *Shen of the Sea.*

TEXT SET:

The Dark-Thirty: Southern Tales of the Supernatural
by Patricia C. McKissack

McKissack says in her author's note that when she was growing up in the South, the half hour just before nightfall was called the dark-thiry. The tales she relates here are "rooted in African American history and the oral storytelling tradition" and "should be shared at that special time when it is neither day nor night." A special feature of *The Dark-Thirty* is the information McKissack gives readers before each story. For example, McKissack explains that the Brotherhood of Sleeping Car Porters was the first all-black union in the United States and was established in 1926. She gives this information before "The 11:59," an eerie tale about the phantom Death Train known in railroad talk as the 11:59.

Other notable stories are "The Woman in the Snow" which comes after a brief description of the Montgomery, Alabama, bus boycott in 1955-56 and "Justice," which comes after a brief description of the Ku Klux Klan.

Zlateh the Goat and Other Stories by Isaac Bashevis Singer

This is a collection of Jewish folktales set in Poland. The folktale "Zlateh the Goat" is about Aaron and his beloved goat Zlateh. Aaron is sent away to sell Zlateh in order to provide the family with money for the festival of Hanukkah. When Aaron and Zlateh are trapped in a snow storm for three days, Zlateh keeps Aaron warm and feeds him with her warm milk.

When Shlemiel Went to Warsaw and Other Stories by Isaac Bashevis Singer

This is an additional collection of Jewish folktales set in Poland. The tale "When Shlemiel Went to Warsaw" finds the foolish Shlemiel leaving his hometown of Chelm and making his way to Warsaw. He unwittingly ends up back in Chelm where he believes he has found an identical family to the one he left behind.

Tales from Silver Lands by Charles J. Finger

Charles J. Finger travelled throughout Central and South America during the 1920's and collected these stories told to him by indigenous natives.

"A Tale of Three Tails" explains how the deer, the rat, and the rabbit came to have tails and how a wicked wizard was turned into an armadillo.

"The Tale of the Lazy People" originated in Colombia and explains the origin of monkeys as well as teaches the lesson "that automation can never substitute for the joy of accomplishing things for oneself."

Anpao: An American Indian Odyssey by Jamake Highwater

Anpao, whose name in Dakota means "dawn," is a composite character Highwater created, as he says, "out of many stories of the boyhood of early Indians, and from my own experience as well, in order to make an Indian 'Ulysses.' The collection of stories tells how 'the boy Anpao was born and of his adventures among the people and among the spirits.' However, it's not necessary to read all of the stories or to read them in a particular order, although understanding the circumstances of Anpao's birth is helpful.

Two especially dramatic stories are "Anpao and the Magic Dogs," a story describing the first horses and the first rifles the Indians encounter, and "He Comes from the East," a Kiowa story that tells of the coming of smallpox to the Indians.

The Cow-Tail Switch and Other West African Stories by Harold Courlander and George Herzog

This collection of West African tales includes the Liberian tale "The Cow-Tail Switch" with its theme "that a man is not really dead until he is forgotten." The Anansi story "Anansi's Fishing Expedition" tells of the trickster figure in the Ashanti culture who is somewhat like the character of Iktomi in the Native American culture (see *Iktomi and the Ducks* — Culminating Activities). Anansi, who in some stories is human and in other stories is a spider, is often clever but at times is tricked himself as in "Anansi's Fishing Expedition."

CULMINATING ACTIVITIES

• Have students read picture books such as Paul Goble's *Iktomi and the Ducks* and *Star Boy* as well as Olaf Baker's *Where the Buffaloes Begin* and Caron Lee Cohen's *The Mud Pony.* Students can discuss how the stories compare and contrast with those in *Anpao.*

• Have students plot on a map of the United States the places that different groups of Native Americans live. (For a more historical look, read *Indian America: A Geography of North American Indians* by Marian Wallace Ney, Cherokee

Publications, P.O. Box 124, Cherokee, NC 28719. Another resource is *American Indian Reference Books for Children and Young Adults* by Barbar J. Kuipers, Libraries Unlimited, Englewood, Colorado, 1991.)

• Have students read other Anansi stories such as Gerald McDermott's *A Story, A Story*, Eric Kimmel's *Anansi and the Moss Covered Rock,* and Verna Aardema's *Anansi Finds a Fool.* Compare them also with the Nicaraguan tale *Brother Anansi and the Cattle Ranch* and the Caribbean tale *Anancy and Mr. Dry Bone* by Fiona French.

Genre: Nonfiction, Biography, and Autobiography

Nonfiction, or informational books, present facts and information about the world's past, present, and future. Biographies are factual accounts of people's lives, whereas autobiographies are factual accounts of people's lives from their points of view. (Note: This type of book for young readers is often referred to as an "autobiographical novel" because the author is represented by the main character.)

Characteristics

• Nonfiction books often contain accurate and detailed information as in *Commodore Perry in the Land of the Shogun.*

• Biographies often contain photographs, historical documents, and significant quotations as in *Lincoln: A Photobiography*.

• Autobiographies are told in the first person as in *The Upstairs Room*.

TEXT SET:
NONFICTION
Sugaring Time by Kathryn Lasky

This photo essay follows Alice and Don Lacey and their three children as they harvest the small sugarbush on their farm. A wonderful blend of the old (the use of Belgian workhorses) and the new (the use of evaporator pans and storage tanks). (*Sugaring Time* would be a nice nonfiction companion to the fiction book *Miracles on Maple Hill.*)

BIOGRAPHY
The Wright Brothers: How They Invented the Airplane
by Russell Freedman

Freedman's gift as an author is that he turns dull facts into interesting reading. This book is additionally appealing because it includes original photographs taken by Wilbur and Orville Wright.

AUTOBIOGRAPHY
The Upstairs Room by Johanna Reiss

Ten-year-old Annie (who represents Reiss) a member of a Dutch-Jewish family during World War II, is hidden for two years along with her sister in a Gentile family's upstairs room. (Note: Reiss' sequel is *The Journey Back*.)

CULMINATING ACTIVITIES
- Suggest that students write their own autobiographies.
- Ask students to interview members of their families or community and write their biographies.
- Have students write information books illustrated with photographs and/or drawings.

ORGANIZING AUTHOR STUDIES

An author study is an in-depth examination of several books written by the same author.

One way of conducting an author study is to have students read all or most of the books in a text set and record responses to their reading in response journals. Teachers often reply to students' response journal entries. Students may also exchange entries with classmates who are reading the same book.

After reading the books in the author study text set, students form literature circles to identify and discuss recurring themes and elements. Groups can create charts that identify and give examples of themes and elements of each book.

Alternatively, have students read one of the books from a text set then follow up with literature circle discussions as described in Chapter 2. Form literature circles consisting of students who have read different books in the text set. Students can discuss elements and themes of each book and summarize information on a chart.

A final activity for both methods of conducting an author study is to have each group create and display a poster of its chart for an all-class comparison-contrast discussion.

Following is a sample chart and text set for a Scott O'Dell author study.

AUTHOR STUDY

Title	Elements: Challenging Physical Environment	Cultural Practices
Island of the Blue Dolphins	Karana must fight wild dogs and endure tropical storms as she struggles to survive.	Although females were not allowed to make weapons or hunt, Karana must do both in order to survive alone on her island.
Sing Down the Moon	Bright Morning is forced to walk 300 miles from her home in Arizona to a reservation at Fort Sumner, New Mexico.	Bright Morning has her Womanhood Ceremony (Kin-nadl -dah).
The Black Pearl	Ramón must survive a thunder storm as well as his encounter with the giant manta ray, El Manta Diablo.	Pearl diving is a part of Ramón's heritage and a part of the culture of the town of La Paz.
The King's Fifth	Estéban must cross the vast desert and plain known as "Despoblado," the "Uninhabited."	Chief Quantah of Nexpan has little use for the gold that Estéban and his group lust for.

SCOTT O'DELL

Intruders	Theme: Personal courage is needed to overcome fear and to live honorably.
Captain Orlov and the Aleuts attack Karana's village. Also, when Karana is alone on the island, the wild dogs are intruders.	Karana learns all the skills necessary to survive on the island. She even makes Rontu-Aru, a wild dog, her friend.
Bright Morning is captured by Spanish slavers. After her return home, she is forced onto a reservation by the federal government.	Bright Morning escapes from the Spanish slavers and also from the reservation at Bosque Redondo.
Ramón must fight Gaspar Ruiz and El Manta Diablo for the Pearl of Heaven.	Ramón says the "beginning day of manhood" was the day he returned from the sea for the second time with the Pearl of Heaven and placed it in the Madonna's hands as a "gift of adoration."
Estéban and his group are the intruders as they search for gold in New Spain.	Estéban chooses to stand trial rather than continue the destructive quest for gold.

TEXT SET:

Island of the Blue Dolphins

Karana is left behind when her people leave the island after being attacked by the Aleut. She courageously learns to shelter herself, make weapons, gather food, and protect herself from wild dogs. (The sequel is *Zia*.)

Sing Down the Moon

Bright Morning is fourteen years old when she is captured by Spanish slavers. Tall Boy helps her escape, but his right arm is crippled during the rescue. Bright Morning returns to her beloved home in the canyon only to be forced onto a reservation 300 miles away.

The Black Pearl

Sixteen-year-old Ramón Salazar overcomes El Manta Diablo, the fearsome manta ray, that guards the precious black pearl known as the Pearl of Heaven. When Ramón suspects that owning the pearl is causing the village and his family harm, he decides to retun it to El Diablo, but Gaspar Ruiz, The Sevillano, wants the pearl for himself.

The King's Fifth

The King's portion of all gold and wealth acquired in the New World is one-fifth and is called "the King's fifth." Estéban de Sandoval, a young Spanish mapmaker, is accused of not paying "the King's fifth" after hiding the gold his expedition, led by the ruthless Captain Mendoza, has gathered in the territories of New Spain. In hiding the gold, Estéban breaks the law but redeems himself.

CHAPTER FOUR

Whole-Group Instruction

Another way you might want to use Newbery books in your classroom is to use a whole-group approach in which all students read the same book and participate in many or all of the same activities.

When implementing this approach, you might find the following three-stage literacy model helpful.

STAGE 1: INTO

Students engage in activities that activate their prior knowledge. "Into" gets students ready to read.

STAGE 2 : THROUGH

Activities help students comprehend what they are reading.

STAGE 3: BEYOND

The final stage extends the literature experience and helps students make connections between the books and other curricular areas.

Following are examples of activities you can implement at each stage using the following books:
- *Lincoln: A Photobiography*
- *Volcano: The Eruption and Healing of Mount St. Helens*
- *Joyful Noise: Poems for Two Voices*

Lincoln: A Photobiography by Russell Freedman

Using photographs and illustrations, including those of documents and artifacts, Russell Freedman introduces students to the 16th president of the United States. While exploring Lincoln's life and career, Freedman also provides an effective, readable description of issues surrounding Lincoln and a country divided by civil war.

STAGE 1:

You may want to begin your whole-group instruction by helping students create a giant K-W-L chart: K-students tell what they know; W-students tell what they want to know; L-students tell what they've learned. Students can use this chart not only at the beginning of a study of Lincoln but also as a concluding activity. As a beginning activity, this chart can help you elicit what students already know about Lincoln and at the same time help you point out the difference between fact and myth.

First, ask students to list what they know about Lincoln (K). Students might do this individually, then form small groups to combine and expand lists. Next have students list things they want to know about Lincoln (W). Display on a classroom wall or bulletin board under the heading "Abraham Lincoln— What We Know/What We Want to Know."

STAGE 2:

Engage students in a variety of activities to help them learn more about the subject. For example:

• Students can create time lines of Lincoln's life and historical events that took place during his lifetime. (Suggestion: Use the software *Timeliner* [Tom Snyder Productions] or rolls of newsprint.)

• Provide large cards for bookmarks. As students come across physical descriptions of Lincoln, they can write the information and page numbers on one side of the cards. Every time a character trait is mentioned, they can write those descriptions and page numbers on the reverse side of the cards.

• Students can create mini-plays incorporating vocabulary words from each chapter. For example, have students act out the word "denounced" as it is used in the sentence: "But many others denounced the president."

STAGE 3:

Complete the K-W-L chart by having students create a class list for the heading "What We've Learned." First, return to the K and W lists. Discuss any misconceptions students had about Lincoln. Did students find answers to their questions from the second list (What We Want to Know)? Add this third list to the class chart on display. Other stage 3 activities include:

• Using descriptions from students' notecards, create a

Character T. Draw a large T-shape on a piece of chart paper. Across the top write Lincoln's name. List Lincoln's traits on the left side of the T and sentences from the book that illustrate or support the trait on the other side.

- Hold a press conference and allow students to take turns playing the part of Lincoln.
- Have students draw political cartoons. Display the cartoons "gallery-style" and invite students to comment and discuss.
- In *Lincoln: A Photobiography,* a series of photographs taken of Lincoln from 1861 through 1865 show the strain the war had on him. In cooperative groups, have students list events (historical and personal) that took place during each of those years. As a class activity, look at each photograph while a student reads aloud the events of each of those years.

ADDITIONAL READING SUGGESTIONS

- *The Boys' War* by Jim Murphy (Clarion Books, 1990)
- *Across Five Aprils* by Irene Hunt (Follett, 1964)
- *Behind the Blue and Gray: The Soldier's Life in the Civil War* by Delia Ray (Lodestar Books, 1991)
- *Gentle Annie: The True Story of a Civil War Nurse* by Mary Francis Shura (Scholastic, 1991)
- *To Be a Slave* by Julius Lester (Scholastic, 1968)

Volcano: The Eruption and Healing of Mount St. Helens by Patricia Lauber

This outstanding photo essay about the 1980 eruption of Mount St. Helens is simply written and easy to understand. Color photographs help illustrate the unique ability that nature has to restore and heal itself after monumental natural disasters.

STAGE 1:

Before having students look at the subject of volcanoes in a scientific way, you may want to have students think about volcanoes in a more literary way by having them write poems or descriptive paragraphs.

For example, Lauber personifies Mount St. Helens in her opening sentences: "For many years the volcano slept. It was silent and still, big and beautiful."

One way to get students ready to write creatively is to use synectics, a creativity strategy that requires students to think about different comparisons.

Below is a synectic exercise you might want to do with your students to elicit vocabulary words they can then incorporate in their poems or descriptive paragraphs.

• How is a volcano like a popcorn popper?
• Pretend you are a volcano getting ready to erupt after sleeping for 200 years. What would you see, hear, smell, feel, and say?
• How is a volcano both beautiful and ugly?

(Note: You might also want to display photographs of volcanoes from Lauber's book, Seymour Simon's book *Volcanoes,* or from the June/July, 1993 issue of *Kids Discover*, which features volcanoes.)

After students complete the exercise and share their descriptive words with others, they can write poems or paragraphs using the title of Lauber's first chapter, "The Volcano Wakes."

STAGE 2:

• Students can create Fast Fact cards that identify important facts from the book. For example: Molten rock inside the volcano is called MAGMA, but molten rock outside the volcanoe is called LAVA.

• Students can pretend to be television reporters and present newscasts that report the events leading up to the eruption, the eruption itself, and what followed the eruption.

• Challenge students to locate Mount St. Helens on a map and point to where the mudflows from the volcano choked the Cowlitz River and blocked channels in the Columbia River.

STAGE 3:

• Let students choose and research other volcanic eruptions such as Iceland's Mount Laki, Indonesia's Krakatau, Hawaii's Kilauea, Philippines' Mount Pinatubo, and Colombia's Nevado del Ruiz.

• Let students identify and locate the countries with the most active volcanoes:

U.S. (including Alaska and Hawaii)	157
Former U.S.S.R.	141
Indonesia	127
Japan	77
Chile	75
Iceland	62
Ethiopia	57
Philippines	51
Papua New Guinea	43
Mexico	31

(Source: *Kids Discover*, June/July, 1993)

• Let students create their own volcanic eruptions or design experiments that demonstrate how volcanoes release sulfur dioxide gas into the air. (Check science books for directions.)

• Create a bulletin board display using news stories about more recent volcanic eruptions such as Mount Pinatubo in the Philippines.

ADDITIONAL READING SUGGESTIONS

The Eruption of Krakatoa by Rupert Matthews (Bookwright Press, 1989)

Experiments That Explore the Greenhouse Effect by Martin J. Gutnik (Millbrook Press, 1991)

Volcanoes by Seymour Simon (Morrow Junior Books, 1988)

The 21 Balloons by William Pene duBois (Dell, 1947)

Volcanoes by Gregory Vogt (Franklin Watts, 1993)

Joyful Noise: Poems for Two Voices by Paul Fleischman

This sensational volume of poetry recreates the "joyful noise" of insects. It's written to be read aloud by two readers at once and can even serve as a wonderful introduction or companion to a science unit on insects.

STAGE 1:

- With a companion, students can perform one or two of the poems from *Joyful Noise*. "Honeybees," "Book Lice," and "Water Boatmen" are especially entertaining.
- Use "I Hate Bugs! I Like Them." from Mary Ann Hoberman's book *Bugs* for a choral reading.

STAGE 2:

- Discuss with students how they can prepare and perform a two-person poem. Note: For a good checklist students can use to help prepare for performances, see *Better Than Book Reports* (Scholastic, 1992)
- Have student pairs choose and perform poems from Newbery winner *Joyful Noise* or *I Am Phoenix*.

STAGE 3:

- Read aloud *The Icky Bug Alphabet Book* and have students choose a bug to research.
- Have student partners choose a type of bug to represent and write and perform a two-person poem. (You might also suggest that students have their bugs represent combinations such as brother-sister, sister-sister, brother-brother, grandmother-granddaughter, and so on)
- Share Chris Van Allsburg's wordless book *Two Bad Ants* (Houghton, Mifflin, 1988) and have students write two-person poems describing the incredible adventure the two ants had while trying to hide away in the home of the sparkling crystals. (Another possibility: The adventurous ants get a lecture from their parents when they return.)

ADDITIONAL READING SUGGESTIONS

Bugs by Mary Ann Hoberman (Viking Press, 1976)
I Am Phoenix: Poems for Two Voices by Paul Fleischman (HarperCollins, 1985)
Never Say Ugh to a Bug by Norma Farber (Greenwillow, 1979)

The Icky Bug Alphabet Book by Jerry Pallotta (Children's Press, 1986)

Hey, Bug! and Other Poems About Little Things by Elizabeth M. Itse (American Heritage Press, 1972)

Where Do They Go? Insects in Winter by Millicent E. Selsam (Four Winds Press, 1982)

CHAPTER FIVE

Independent Reading

Motivating students to read because they *want* to read is at the heart of any independent reading program. An independent reading program that accomplishes this goal usually depends upon three factors: enthusiasm, opportunity, and guidance.

ENTHUSIASM

With more than 300 titles in the Newbery collection, you and your students are sure to be enthused about a number of different books, authors, and genres. Following are suggestions for encouraging this enthusiasm in your independent reading program:

- Share books that you own. Promote student ownership as well.
- Talk about books—bring titles and authors up in conversations; ask students about books they're reading.
- Let students see you read.
- Read books aloud to students.
- Respect students' choices but also recommend additional titles and authors.

OPPORTUNITY

What do successful student independent reading programs have in common? Access to good, quality books such as Newbery books.

Following are some tips for stocking your classroom library:

- Check garage and rummage sales for used books;
- shop for books at used book stores;
- buy books at library book sales;
- start a "Buy a Book Birthday Club" where students add their favorite paperback book to the classroom library on their birthdays; (create book plates recognizing the donors);
- use extra points from book club orders to purchase books for your classroom library;
- invite parents to help (they might donate books their children have read, loan some family favorites, or donate a special title);

• rotate a section of books from your school or community libraries.

It's also helpful to keep up on what's available at your school and community libraries so you can point students in the right direction when they ask about books or want a recommendation. Most community libraries have Newbery book collections in both paperback and hard cover. Some libraries shelve Newbery books in a special section. Finally, you might ask your community librarian or school media specialist/librarian to tell you which Newbery books are available in paperback, hard bound, or both, thus helping you wisely spend your money for the purchase of Newbery books.

GUIDANCE

Many students benefit from guidance in selecting books to read independently. Below are some strategies you might use to help your students select books that are well-matched to their abilities and interest.

Abandon Book!

Many teachers suggest that students abandon books and select others if they don't like their choices after reading an agreed-upon number of pages. (I abandon a book if I'm not interested after reading the first chapter; however, I know other teachers who require students to read the first 50 pages before abandoning a book.) Discuss the idea with your students. Do they ever abandon a book? Do you? Why? After how many pages? Based on the experiences of all class readers, establish a policy.

Revisit a Book

We all have favorite books we like to reread every once in a while, and students are no different. Consequently, because the Newbery collection is so varied and populated with such interesting characters, you may support older elementary students in "revisiting" old classics such as *Charlotte's Web*.

Although technically a "revisited book" is one students are rereading, abandoned books can turn into revisited books if students decide they are ready to read them.

Five Fingers to Self-Selection

Often students become discouraged with books because they select books that are too difficult. The "Five Finger" method described here can help students judge for themselves if a book is too difficult:

1. The student selects a 100-word passage from the book. (Have the student count the number of words so the test is accurate.)

2. The student reads the passage aloud to you or to a fellow student.

3. The student raises one finger every time a difficult word is encountered (can't pronounce or doesn't understand).

4. If, at the end of the passage, the student has all five fingers raised, the book is probably too difficult.

5. If students insist on reading books that may be too difficult, let them. Sometimes students choose difficult books on purpose and struggle with them. At a later date, however, they may return to the same books and read them much more easily.

The Goldilocks Strategy

Classroom teacher Mary Jepsen developed the Goldilocks Strategy to help students identify books that are too difficult, too easy, or just right for them. (The strategy is playfully named, of course, after Goldilocks, who sampled porridge that was too hot, too cold, and just right.)

Too Hard: A book a student may want to read, which is too difficult right now. The book contains too many words the student does not know yet (see "Five Finger" method above). Sometimes "Too Hard" books are long and/or have smaller type.

Too Easy: This can be a book the student has read before without difficulty. (Students can be encouraged to read these books as a "break" between more challenging reading.)

Just Right: "Just Right" books may contain one or two new words per page and are challenging enough to hold the reader's attention without being frustrating.

Before using this strategy with your students, first model the three levels by sharing books that are too difficult, too easy, and just right. For example, you might read from a technical book such as a biotechnology textbook as an example of a book that fits into the "too hard" category. A simple, pre-school picture book may fit the "too easy" category. Finally, you might share a passage read from a novel you are reading as an example of a book that is "just right" for you.

JUDGING A BOOK BY ITS COVER

Students who are browsing for books and do not have specific titles or authors in mind might choose books because of their cover art and the story descriptions that appear either inside the jacket cover or on the back of the book itself.

Because cover art influences student choices, sometimes really good books get passed over because their cover art isn't as appealing as that of others. For example, the pale, sketchy art on the cover of *The Hundred Dresses* may not be as appealing to many students as the bold, revealing portrait on the cover of *The Great Gilly Hopkins.*

By showing students several examples of books that can't be judged by their covers (especially if the book is an older, ragged, hard bound copy), you can help students develop strategies for making good book choices.

Buddy Reading

With buddy reading, two or more students read the same title at the same time (each with his own copy). Students who "buddy read" encourage one another and can ask each other questions if they don't understand something. They can also share and respond to favorite passages or events. In other words, buddy reading is an example of a very informal literature circle comprised of two people.

Hooked on a Series or Author

As mentioned in Chapter 1, you can encourage students to read independently by getting them interested in reading a book series or books written by a particular author.

Following is a list of books related to Newbery Award and Honor books. In addition to encouraging students to read Newbery books, you can also encourage students to read other book series by Newbery-award-winning authors such Betsy Byars and Lois Lowry.

Note: * indicates Newbery book

Lloyd Alexander (Chronicles of Prydain)

Book of Three (Holt, 1964)
The Black Cauldron (Holt, 1965)*
Castle of Llyr (Holt, 1966)
Tartan Wanderer (Holt, 1967)
The High King (Holt, 1968)*

William H. Armstrong

Sounder (Harper, 1969)*
Sour Land (Harper, 1971)

Carol Ryrie Brink

Caddie Woodlawn (Macmillan, 1935)*
Magical Melons (Macmillan, 1944)

Beverly Cleary

Dear Mr. Henshaw (Morrow, 1983)*
Strider (Morrow, 1991)
Ramona and Her Father (Morrow, 1977)*
Ramona and Her Mother (Morrow, 1979)
Ramona Quimby, Age 8 (Morrow, 1981)*
Ramona Forever (Morrow, 1984)

Eleanor Estes

Ginger Pye (Harcourt, 1951)*
Pinky Pye (Harcourt, 1958)
Moffats (Harcourt, 1941)
Middle Moffat (Harcourt, 1942)*
Rufus M (Harcourt, 1943)*

Moffat Museum (Harcourt, 1983)

Paul Fleischman

I Am Phoenix: Poems for Two Voices (Harper, 1985)
Joyful Noise: Poems for Two Voices (Harper, 1988)*

Jean Craighead George

My Side of the Mountain (Dutton, 1967)*
On the Far Side of the Mountain (Dutton, 1990)

Bette Greene

Philip Hall Likes Me, I Reckon Maybe (Dial, 1974)*
Get On Out of Here, Philip Hall (Bantam, 1978)

Marguerite Henry

Misty of Chincoteague (Rand McNally, 1947)*
Sea Star (Randy McNally, 1949)
Stormy, Misty's Foal (Rand McNally, 1963)

Robert Lawson

Rabbit Hill (Viking, 1944)*
Tough Winter (Viking, 1954)

Madeleine L'Engle (Time Series)

A Wrinkle in Time (Farrar, 1962)*
A Wind in the Door (Farrar, 1973)
A Swiftly, Tilting Planet (Farrar, 1978)
Many Waters (Farrar, 1986)

Cynthia Voight (Tillerman Saga)

Homecoming (Atheneum, 1981)
Dicey's Song (Atheneum, 1984)*
Solitary Blue (Atheneum, 1983)*
Come a Stranger (Atheneum, 1986)
Sons from Afar (Atheneum, 1987)
17 Against the Dealer (Atheneum, 1989)

Scott O'Dell

Island of the Blue Dolphins (Houghton, 1960)*
Zia (Houghton, 1976)

Gary Paulsen

Hatchet (Bradbury, 1987)*
The River (Delacorte, 1991)

George Selden

Cricket in Times Square (Farrar, 1960)*
Tucker's Countryside (Farrar, 1969)
Harry Cat's Pet Puppy (Farrar, 1974)
Chester Cricket's Pigeon Ride (Farrar, 1981)
Chester Cricket's New Home (Farrar, 1983)

Mildred D. Taylor (Logan Family Series)

Song of the Trees (Dial, 1975)
Roll of Thunder, Hear My Cry (Dial, 1976)*
Let the Circle Be Unbroken (Dial, 1981)
The Friendship (Dial, 1987)
The Road to Memphis (Dial, 1990)
Mississippi Bridge (Dial, 1990)

Laura Ingalls Wilder (Little House Series)

Little House in the Big Woods (Harper, 1932)
Little House on the Prairie (Harper, 1935)
Farmer Boy (Harper, 1933)
On the Banks of Plum Creek (Harper, 1937)*
By the Shores of Silver Lake (Harper, 1939)*
The Long Winter (Harper, 1940)*
Little Town on the Prairie (Harper, 1941)*
These Happy, Golden Years (Harper, 1943)*
First Four Years (Harper, 1971)

BIBLIOGRAPHY: PROFESSIONAL RESOURCES

Anderson, Vicki. *Fiction Sequels for Readers 10 to 16.* Jefferson, North Carolina: McFarland & Company, Inc., 1990.

Bromley Karen. *Journaling* New York: Scholastic, 1993

Chertok, Bobbi, Hirshfeld, Goody, and Rosh, Marilyn. *Meet the Masterpieces.* New York: Scholastic, 1992.

Daniels, Harvey. *Collaborative Reading: Literature Circles and Text Sets in the Classroom.* (in press; publication information unavailable at press time).

Flanagan, Marianne. "Starting Literature Circles in Fifth Grade." *Best Practice.* National-Lewis University Chicago Project on Learning and Teaching, Vol. 2, 1991: page 4.

Kuipers, Barbara J. *American Indian Reference Books for Children and Young Adults.* Englewood, Colorado: Libraries Unlimited, 1991.

Moen, Christine Boardman. *Better Than Book Reports.* New York: Scholastic, 1992.

Ney, Marian Wallace. *Indian America: A Geography of North American Indians.* Cherokee, N.C., 1986.

Ohlhausen, Marilyn M. and Jepsen, Mary. "Lessons from Goldilocks: 'Somebody's Been Choosing My Books But I Can Make My Own Choices Now!' *The New Advocate.* (Volume 5, Winter, 1992): pages 31-46.

Peterson, Ralph and Eeds, Maryann. *Grand Conversations: Literature Groups in Action.* New York: Scholastic, 1990.

Rosenberg, Judith K. *Young People's Books in Series.* Englewood, Colorado: Libraries Unlimited, Inc., 1992.

Routman, Regie. *Invitations: Changing as Teachers and Learners*. Portsmouth: Heinemann 1991.

Schell, Leo. *How to Create an Independent Reading Program*. New York: Scholastic, 1991.

Short, Kathy Gnagey and Pierce, Kathryn Mitchell. *Talking About Books: Creating Literate Communities*. Portsmouth: Heinemann, 1990.

Sutherland, Zena and Arbuthrot, Mary Hill. *Children and Books*. New York: Harper Collins, 1991.

Wollman-Bonilla, Julie. *Response Journals*. New York: Scholastic, 1991.

Complete List of Newbery Medal and Honor Books, 1922-1993

1993

Winner: *Missing May*. (Orchard) Cynthia Rylant

Honors: *The Dark-Thirty*. (Knopf) Patricia McKissack
Somewhere in the Darkness. (Scholastic) Walter Dean Myers
What Hearts. (HarperCollins) Bruce Brooks

1992

Winner: *Shiloh*. (Dell) Phyllis Reynolds Naylor

Honors: *The Wright Brothers*. (Holiday) Russell Freedman
Nothing but the Truth. (Orchard) Avi

1991

Winner: *Maniac Magee*. (Little) Jerry Spinelli

Honors: *True Confessions of Charlotte Doyle*. (Orchard) Avi

1990

Winner: *Number the Stars*. (Houghton) Lois Lowry

Honors: *Afternoon of the Elves*. (Orchard) Janet Taylor Lise;
The Winter Room. (Orchard) Gary Paulsen; *Shabanu: Daughter
of the Wind*. (Knopf) Suzanne Fisher Staples

1989

Winner: *Joyful Noise: Poems for Two Voices*. (Harper & Row)
Paul Fleischman

Honors: *In the Beginning: Creation Stories from Around the
World* (Harcourt) Virginia Hamilton; *Scorpions*. (Harper) Walter
Dean Myers

1988

Winner: *Lincoln: A Photobiography*. (Clarion) Russell Freedman

Honors: *After the Rain*. (Morrow) Norma Fox Mazer; *Hatchet*. (Bradbury) Gary Paulsen

1987

Winner: *The Whipping Boy*. (Greenwillow) Sid Fleischman

Honors: *On My Honor*. (Clarion) Marion Dane Bauer; *Volcano: The Eruption and Healing of Mount St. Helens*. (Bradbury) Patricia Lauber; *A Fine White Dust*. (Bradbury) Cynthia Rylant

1986

Winner: *Sarah, Plain and Tall*. (Harper Jr.) Patricia MacLachlan

Honors: *Commodore Perry in the Land of the Shogun*. (Lothrop) Rhoda Blumberg; *Dogsong*. (Bradbury) Gary Paulsen

1985

Winner: *The Hero and the Crow*. (Greenwillow) Robin McKinley

Honors: *The Moves Make the Man*. (Harper) Bruce Brooks; *The One-Eyed Cat*. (Bradbury) Paula Fox; *Like Jake and Me*. (Knopf) Mavis Jukes

1984

Winner: *Dear Mr. Henshaw*. (Morrow) Beverly Cleary

Honors: *The Wish Giver*. (Harper) Bill Brittain; *Sugaring Time* (Macmillan) Kathryn Lasky; *The Sign of the Beaver*. (Houghton) Elizabeth George Speare; *A Solitary Blue*. (Atheneum) Cynthia Voigt

1983

Winner: *Dicey's Song.* (Atheneum) Cynthia Voigt

Honors: *Graven Images.* (Harper) Paul Fleischman; *Homesick: My Own Story.* (Putnam) Jean Fritz; *Sweet Whispers, Brother Rush.* (Philomel) Virginia Hamilton; *The Blue Sword.* (Greenwillow) Robin McKinley; *Doctor De Soto.* (Farrar) William Steig

1982

Winner: *A Visit to William Blake's Inn: Poems for Innocent and Experienced Travelers.* (Harcourt) Nancy Willard

Honors: *Ramona Quimby, Age 8.* (Morrow) Beverly Cleary; *Upon the Head of the Goat: A Childhood in Hungary 1939-1944.* (Farrar) Aranka Siegal

1981

Winner: *Jacob Have I Loved.* (Crowell) Katherine Paterson *The Fledgling* (Harper) Jane Langton; *A Ring of Endless Light.* (Farrar) Madeleine L'Engle

1980

Winner: *A Gathering of Days: A New England Girl's Journal, 1830-32.* (Scribner) Joan W. Blos

Honors: *The Road from Home: The Story of an Armenian Girl.* (Greenwillow) David Kheridian

1979

Winner: *The Westing Game.* (Dutton) Ellen Raskin *The Great Gilly Hopkins.* (Crowell) Katherine Paterson

1978

Winner: *Bridge to Terabithia.* (Crowell) Katherine Paterson

Honors: *Ramona and Her Father.* (Morrow) Beverly Cleary; *Anpao: An American Indian Odyssey.* (Lippincott) Jamake Highwater

1977

Winner: *Roll of Thunder, Hear My Cry.* (Dial) Mildred D. Taylor

Honors: *A String in the Harp.* (Atheneum) Nancy Bond *Abel's Island.* (Farrar) William Steig

1976

Winner: *The Grey King.* (Atheneum) Susan Cooper

Honors: *The Hundred Penny Box.* (Viking) Sharon Bell Mathis; *Dragonwings.* (Harper) Laurence Yep

1975

Winner: *M.C. Higgins, The Great.* (Macmillan) Virginia Hamilton

Honors: *My Brother Sam is Dead.* (Four Winds) James Lincoln; Collier and Christopher Collier; *Philip Hall Likes Me, I Reckon Maybe.* (Dial) Bette Greene; *The Perilous Gard.* (Houghton) Elizabeth Marie Pope; *Figgs and Phantoms.* (Dutton) Ellen Raskin

1974

Winner: *The Slave Dancer.* (Bradbury) Paula Fox *The Dark is Rising.* (Atheneum) Susan Cooper

1973

Winner: *Julie of the Wolves*. (Harper) Jean Craighead George

Honors: *Frog and Toad Together*. (Harper) Arnold Lobel; *The Upstairs Room*. (Crowell) Johanna Reiss; *The Witches of Worm*. (Atheneum) Zilpha Keatley Snyder

1972

Winner: *Mrs. Frisby and the Rats of NIMH*. (Atheneum) Robert C. O'Brien

Honors: *Incident at Hawk's Hill*. (Little, Brown) Allan W. Eckert; *The Planet of Junior Brown*. (Macmillan) Virginia Hamilton; *The Tombs of Atuan*. (Atheneum) Ursula K. Le Guin; *Annie and the Old One*. (Little) Miska Miles; *The Headless Cupid*. (Atheneum) Zilpha Keatley Snyder

1971

Winner: *Summer of the Swans*. (Viking) Betsy Byars; *Knee Knock Rise*. (Farrar) Natalie Babbitt; *Enchantress from the Stars*. (Atheneum) Sylvia Louise Engdahl; *Sing Down the Moon*. (Houghton) Scott O'Dell

1970

Winner: *Sounder*. (Harper) William H. Armstrong *Our Eddie*. (Pantheon) Sulamith Ish-Kishor *The Many Ways of Seeing: An Introduction to the Pleasures of Art*. (World) Janet Gaylor Moore *Journey Outside*. (Viking) Mary Q. Steele

1969

Winner: *The High King*. (Holt) Lloyd Alexander; *To Be a Slave*. (Dial) Julius Lester; *When Shlemiel Went to Warsaw and Other Stories*. (Farrar) Isaac Bashevis Singer

1968

Winner: *From the Mixed-Up Files of Mrs. Basil E. Frankweiler.* (Atheneum) E. L. Konigsburg

Honors: *Jennifer, Hecate, MacBeth, William McKinley, and Me Elizabeth.* (Atheneum) E. L. Konigsburg; *The Black Pearl.* (Houghton) Scott O'Dell; *The Fearsome Inn.* (Scribner) Isaac Bashevis Singer; *The Egypt Gam.e* (Atheneum) Zilpha Keatley Snyder

1967

Winner: *Up a Road Slowly.* (Follet) Irene Hunt

Honors: *The King's Fifth.* (Houghton) Scott O'Dell *Zlateh the Goat and Other Stories.* (Harper) Isaac Bashevis Singer *The Jazz Man.* (Atheneum) Mary Hays Weik

1966

Winner: *I, Juan De Pareja.* (Farrar) Elizabeth Borton de Trevino

Honors: *The Black Cauldron.* (Holt) Lloyd Alexander; *The Animal Family.* (Pantheon) Randall Jarrell; *The Noonday Friends.* (Harper) Mary Stolz

1965

Winner: *Shadow of a Bull.* (Atheneum) Maia Wojciechowska

Honors: *Across Five Aprils.* (Follett) Irene Hunt

1964

Winner: *It's Like This, Cat.* (Harper) Emily Neville

Honors: *Rascal.* (Dutton) Sterling North; *The Loner.* (McKay) Ester Wier

1963

Winner: *A Wrinkle in Time.* (Farrar) Madeleine L'Engle

Honors: *Thistle and Thyme; Tale and Legends from Scotland.* (Holt) Sorche Nic Leodhas, pseudonym for Leclaire Alger; *Men of Athens.* (Houghton) Olivia Coolidge

1962

Winner: *The Bronze Bow.* (Houghton) Elizabeth George Speare

Honors: *Frontier Living.* (World) Edwin Tunis; *The Golden Goblet.* (Coward) Eloise Jarvis McGraw; *Belling the Tiger.* (Harper) Mary Stolz

1961

Winner: *Island of the Blue Dolphins.* (Houghton) Scott O'Dell

Honors: *America Moves Forward.* (Morrow) Gerald W. Johnson *Old Ramon.* (Houghton) Jack Schaefer *Cricket in Times Square.* (Farrar, Straus) George Selden, pseudonym for George Thompson

1960

Winner: *Onion John.* (Crowell) Joseph Krumgold

Honors: *My Side of the Mountain.* (Dutton) Jean Craighead George; *America Is Born.* (Morrow) Gerald W. Johson; *The Gammage Cup.* (Harcourt) Carol Kendall

1959

Winner: *The Witch of Blackbird Pond.* (Houghton) Elizabeth George Speare

Honors: *The Family Under the Bridge.* (Harper) Natalie S. Carlson; *Along Came a Dog.* (Harper) Meindert DeJong; *Chucaro: Wild*

Pony of the Pampa. (Harcourt Francis) Kalnay; *The Perilous Road.* (Harcourt) William O. Steele

1958

Winner: *Rifles for Watie.* (Crowell) Harold Keith

Honors: *Gone-Away Lake.* (Harcourt) Elizabeth Enright *Tom Paine, Freedom's Apostle.* (Crowell) Leo Gurke; *The Great Wheel.* (Viking) Robert Lawson; *The Horse Catcher.* (Westminster) Mari Sandoz

1957

Winner: *Miracles on Maple Hill.* (Harcourt) Virginia Sorensen

Honors: *Black Fox of Lorne.* (Doubleday) Marguerite de Angeli; *The House of Sixty Fathers.* (Harper) Meindert DeJong; *Old Yeller.* (Harper) Fred Gipson; *Mr. Justice Holmes.* (Follett) Clara Ingram Judson; *The Corn Grows Ripe.* (Viking) Dorothy Rhoads

1956

Winner: *Carry on, Mr. Bowditch.* (Houghton) Jean Lee Latham

Honors: *The Golden Name Day.* (Harper) Jennie Lindquist; *The Secret River.* (Scribner) Marjorie Kinnan Rawlings; *Men, Microscopes, and Living Things.* (Viking) Katherine Shippen

1955

Winner: *The Wheel on the School.* (Harper) Meindert DeJong

Honors: *Courage of Sarah Noble.* (Scribner) Alice Dalgliesh; *Banner in the Sky.* (Lippincott) James Ullman

1954

Winner: *...And Now Miguel.* (Crowell) Joseph Krumgold

Honors: *All Alone.* (Viking) Claire Huchet Bishop; *Magic Maze.* (Houghton) Mary and Conrad Buff; *Hurry Home Candy.* (Harper) Meindert DeJong; *Shadrach.* (Harper) Meindert DeJong; *Theodore Roosevelt, Fighting Patriot.* (Follett) Clara Ingram Judson

1953

Winner: *Secret of the Andes.* (Viking) Ann Nolan Clark

Honors: *The Bears on Hemlock Mountain.* (Scribner) Alice Dalgliesh *Birthdays of Freedom.* (Vol I). (Scribner) Genevieve Foster *Moccasin Trail.* (Coward) Eloise Jarvis McGraw; *Red Sails to Capri.* (Viking) Ann Weil; *Charlotte's Web.* (Harper) E. B. White

1952

Winner: *Ginger Pye.* (Harcourt) Eleanor Estes

Honors: *Americans Before Columbus.* (Viking) Elizabeth Baity; *The Apple and the Arrow.* (Houghton) Mary and Contrad Buff; *Minn of the Mississippi.* (Houghton) Holling C. Holling; *The Defender.* (Scribner) Nicholas Kalashnikoff; *The Light at Tern Rocks.* (Viking) Julie Sauer

1951

Winner: *Amos Fortune, Free Man.* (Dutton) Elizabeth Yates

Honors: *Gandhi, Fighter Without a Sword.* (Morrow) Jeanette Eaton; *Better Known as Johnny Appleseed.* (Lippincott) Mabel Leigh Hunt; *Abraham Lincoln, Friend of the People.* (Follett) Clara Ingram Judson; *The Story of Appleby Capple.* (Harper) Anne Parrish

1950

Winner: *The Door in the Wall.* (Doubleday) Marguerite de Angeli

Honors: *Story of the Negro.* (Knopf) Arna Bontemps; *My Father's Dragon.* (Random House) Ruth Gannett; *Seabird.* (Houghton) Holling C. Holling; *Daughter of the Mountain.* (Viking) Louise Rankin

1948

Winner: *The Twenty-One Balloons.* (Viking) William Pene du Bois

Honors: *The Quaint and Curious Quest of Johnny Longfoot.* (Bobbs Merrill) Catherine Besterman *Pancakes—Paris.* (Viking) Claire Huchet Bishop; *The Cow-Tail Switch, and Other West African Stories.* (Holt) Harold Courlander; *Li Lun, Lad of Courage.* (Abingdon) Carolyn Treffinger; *Misty of Chincoteague.* (Rand McNally) Marguerite Henry

1947

Winner: *Miss Hickory.* (Viking) Carolyn Sherwin Bailey

Honors: *Wonderful Years.* (Messner) Nancy Barnes; *Big Tree.* (Viking) Mary and Conrad Buff; *The Avion My Uncle Flew.* (Appleton) Cyrus Fisher, pseudonym for Darwin L. Teilhet; *The Heavenly Tenants.* (Harper) William Maxwell; *The Hidden Treasure of Glaston.* (Viking) Elanore Jewett

1946

Winner: *Strawberry Girl.* (Lippincott) Lois Lenski

Honors: *Justin Morgan Had a Horse.* (Randy McNally) Marguerite Henry; *The Moved-Outsiders.* (Houghton) Florence Crannel Means; *New Found World.* (Viking) Katherine Shippen; *Bhimsa, The Dancing Bear.* (Scribner) Christine Weston

1945

Winner: *Rabbit Hill.* (Viking) Robert Lawson

Honors: *The Silver Pencil.* (Scribner) Alice Dalgliesh; *Lone Journey: The Life of Roger Williams.* (Harcourt) Jeannette Eaton; *The Hundred Dresses.* (Harcourt) Eleanor Estes; *Abraham Lincoln's World.* (Scribner) Genevieve Foster

1944

Winner: *Johnny Tremain.* (Houghton) Esther Forbes

Honors: *Rufus M.* (Harcourt) Eleanor Estes; *Fog Magic.* (Viking) Julia Sauer; *These Happy Golden Years.* (Harper) Laura Ingalls Wilder; *Mountain Born.* (Coward) Elizabeth Yates

1943

Winner: *Adam of the Road.* (Viking) Elizabeth Janet Gray

Honors: *The Middle Moffat.* (Harcourt) Eleanor Estes; *"Have You Seen Tom Thumb?"* (Lippincott) Mabel Leigh Hunt

1942

Winner: *The Matchlock Gun.* (Dodd) Walter Edmonds

Honors: *George Washington's World.* (Scribner) Genevieve Foster; *Down Ryton Water.* (Viking) Eva Roe Gaggin; *Indian Captive: The Story of Mary Jemison.* (Lippincott) Lois Lenski ; *Little Town on the Prarie.* (Harper) Laura Ingalls Wilder

1941

Winner: *Call It Courage.* (Macmillan) Armstrong Sperry

Honors: *Young Mac of Fort Vancouver.* (Crowell) Mary Jane Carr; *Blue Willow.* (Viking) Doris Gates; *Nansen.* (Viking) Anna Gertrude Hall; *The Long Winter.* (Harper) Laura Ingalls Wilder

1940

Winner: *Boy with a Pack.* (Harcourt) Stephen W. Meader

Honors: *Runner of the Mountain Tops.* (Randon House) Mabel Robinson; *The Singing Tree.* (Viking) Kate Seredy; *By the Shores of Silver Lake.* (Harper) Laura Ingalls Wilder

1939

Winner: *Thimble Summer.* (Farrar and Rinehart) Elizabeth Enright

Honors: *Nino.* (Viking) Valenti Angelo; *Mr. Popper's Penguins.* (Little, Brown) Richard and Florence Atwater ; *"Hello the Boat!"* (Holt) Phyllis Crawford; *Leader by Destiny: George Washington, Man andPatriot.* (Harcourt) Jeanette Eaton; *Penn.* (Viking) Elizabeth Janet Gray

1938

Winner: *The White Stag.* (Viking) Kate Seredy

Honors: *Pecos Bill.* (Little, Brown) James Cloyd Bowman; *Bright Island.* (Random) Mabel Robinson; *On the Banks of Plum Creek.* (Harper) Laura Ingalls Wilder

1937

Winner: *Roller Skates.* (Viking) Ruth Sawyer

Honors: *Golden Basket.* (Viking) Ludwig Bemelmans; *Winterbound.* (Viking) Margery Bianco; *The Codfish Market.* (Doubleday) Agnes Hewes ;*Whistler's Van.* (Viking) Idwal Jones; *Phebe Fairchild: Her Book.* (Stokes) Lois Lenski; *Audubon.* (Harcourt) Constance Rourke

1936

Winner: *Caddie Woodlawn.* (Macmillan) Carol Ryrie Brink

Honors: *Young Walter Scott.* (Viking) Elizabeth Janet Gray; *The Good Master.* (Viking) Kate Seredy; *All Sail Set.* (Winston) Armstrong Sperry; *Hone, the Moose.* (Dodd) Phil Strong

1935

Winner: *Dobry.* (Viking) Monica Shannon

Honors: *Davy Crockett.* (Harcourt) Constance Rourke *Pageant of Chinese History.* (Longmans) Elizabeth Seeger; *Day on Skates.* (Harper) Hilda Van Stockum

1934

Winner: *Invincible Louisa.* (Little) Cornelia Meigs

Honors: *Winged Girl of Knossos.* (Appleton) Eric Berry, pseudonym for Allena Best; *Big Tree of Bunlahy.* (Macmillan) Padraic Colum; *ABC Bunny.* Wanda Gag; (Coward) *Glory of the Seas.* Agnes Hewes; (Knopf) *Apprentice of Florence.* (Houghton) Anne Kyle; *New Land.* (McBride) Sarah Schmidt; *Swords of Steel.* (Houghton) Elsie Singmaster; *The Forgotten Daughter.* (Doubleday) Caroline Snedeker

1933

Winner: *Young Gu of the Upper Yangtze.* (Winston) Elizabeth Lewis

Honors: *Children of the Soil.* (Doubleday) Nora Burglon; *Swift Rivers.* (Little) Cornelia Meigs; *The Railroad to Freedom.* (Harcourt) Hildegarde Swift

1932

Winner: *Waterless Mountain.* (Longmans) Laura Adams Armer

Honors: *Jane's Island.* (Houghton) Marjorie Allee; *Truce of the Wolf and Other Tales of Old Italy.* (Harcourt) Mary Gould Davis; *Calico Bush.* (Macmillan) Rachel Field; *The Fairy Circus.* (Macmillan) Dorothy Lathrop; *Out of the Flame.* (Longmans) Eloise Lownsbery; *Boy of the South Seas.* (Coward-McCann)Eunice Tietjens

1931

Winner: *The Cat Who Went to Heaven.* (Macmillan) Elizabeth Coatsworth

Honors: *Mountain Are Free.* (Dutton) Julia Davis Adams; *Garram the Hunter.* (Doubleday) Herbert Best; *Meggy MacIntosh.* (Doubleday) Elizabeth Janet; Gray *Spice and the Devil's Cave.* (Knopf) Agnes Hewes; *Queer Person.* (Doubleday) Ralph Hubbard; *Ood-Le-Uk the Wanderer.* (Little) Alice Lide and Margaret Johansen; *The Dark Star of Itza.* (Harcourt) *Foating Island.* (Harper) Anne Parrish

1930

Winner: *Hitty, Her First Hundred Years.* (Macmillan) Rachel Field

Honors: *Vaino.* (Dutton) Julia Davis Adams; *Daughter of the Seine.* (Harper) Jeanette Eaton; *Jumping-Off Place.* (Longmans) Marian Hurd McNeely; *Pran of Albania.* (Doubleday) Elizabeth Miller; *Little Blacknose.* (Harcourt) Hildegarde Swift; *Tangle-Coated Horse and Other Tales.* (Longmans) Ella Young

1929

Winner: *The Trumpeter of Krakow.* (Macmillan) Eric P. Kelly

Honors: *Pigtail of Ah Lee Ben Loo.* (Longmans) John Bennett

Millions of Cats. (Coward) Wanda Gag; *The Boy Who Was.* (Dutton) Grace Hallock; *Clearing Weather.* (Little) Cornelia Meigs; *Runaway Papoose.* (Doubleday) Grace Moon; *Tod of the Fens.* (Macmillan) Elinor Whitney

1928

Winner: *Gay Neck, The Story of a Pigeon.* (Dutton) Dhan Gopal Mukerji

Honors: *Downright Dencey.* (Doubleday) Caroline Snedeker; *The Wonder Smith and His Son.* (Longmans) Ella Young

1927

Winner: *Smoky, the Cowhorse.* (Scribner) Will James

Honors: No Record

1926

Winner: *Shen of the Sea.* (Dutton) Arthur Bowie Crisman

Honors: *Voyagers.* (Macmillan) Padraic Colum

1925

Winner: *Tales from Silver Lands.* (Doubleday) Charles Finger

Honors: *Nicholas.* (Putnam) Anne Carroll Moore; *Dream Coach.* (Macmillan) Anne Parrish

1924

Winner: *The Dark Frigate.* (Little) Charles Hawes

Honors: No Record

1923

Winner: *The Voyages of Doctor Dolittle.* (Lippincott) Hugh Lofting

Honors: No Record

1922

Winner: *The Story of Mankind.* (Liveright) Hendrik Willem van Loon

Honors: *The Old Tobacco Shop.* (Macmillan) William Bowen; *The Golden Flece and the Heroes Who Lived Before Achilles.* (Macmillan) Padraic Colum; *The Great Quest.* (Little) Charles Hawes; *Cedric the Forester.* (Appleton) Bernard Marshall; *Windy Hill.* (Macmillan) Cornelia Meigs

NOTES

NOTES

NOTES

NOTES

NOTES